Gift
of
Joanna White

THE INNOCENT ASSASSINS

WITH DRAWINGS BY

Laszlo Kubinyi

CHARLES SCRIBNER'S SONS / *New York*

THE
INNOCENT
ASSASSINS

LOREN EISELEY

PRINTED IN THE UNITED STATES OF AMERICA
Library of Congress Catalog Card Number 73–5182
SBN 684-13525-6 (cloth)

To the bone hunters of the old South Party,
Morrill Expeditions 1931–1933,
and to C. Bertrand Schultz,
my comrade of those years,
this book in memory of
the unreturning days

CONTENTS

PREFACE

As is readily observable, these are the poems of a bone hunter and a naturalist, or at least those themes are predominant in the book. Some have called me Gothic in my tastes. Others have chosen to regard me as a Platonist, a mystic, a concealed Christian, a midnight optimist. Like most poets I am probably all these things by turns, or such speculations are read into me by those who are pursuing some night path of their own.

As the spokesman in the poem, "Deep in the Grotto," I merely answer that I have been many things. One observation I may perhaps be permitted. Robert Louis Stevenson once remarked that some landscapes cry out for a story. W. H. Hudson found it so of the South American pampas. Though he immigrated in his young manhood to London, his best work continued to revolve about South American themes. Charles Dickens, though he achieved wealth and comfort, was haunted by "the cold, wet, shelterless streets of London." Thoreau never escaped the canopy of the great eastern forest.

I, by contrast, was born on the Great Plains and was drawn almost mesmerically into its rougher margins, the Wild Cat Hills and the Badlands, where bone hunting was a way of life. Few outside the profession of paleontology realize that the eroded areas called "Mauvaises Terres" on the maps of the old voyageurs contain the finest Tertiary fossil beds to be found anywhere in the world. Most of our knowledge of the successive American faunas is derived from excavations in those sterile, sun-washed regions. As a young man engaged in such work, my mind was imprinted by the visible evidence of time and change of enormous magnitude. To me time was never a textbook abstraction. Its remnants lay openly about me in arroyos, in the teetering, eroded pinnacles of Toadstool Park, or farther north in the dinosaur beds of Wyoming. Finally, through some strange mental osmosis these extinct, fragmented creatures merged with and became part of my own identity.

Certainly in body and mind we have been many things, but the story is not fantasy. It lies written in exposed rock and strewn across old tablelands. To me, who, through the vicissitudes of youth, was drawn early into that haunted country, it was impossible not to leave a personal record beyond what was shipped and, for all I know, may still be lying in its stone matrix in museum basements. I was one of the bone hunters, but I was also something else, a fugitive assuming the animal masks of many ages. How this occurred I am not sufficiently articulate to explain. Perhaps I came closest to doing so in my previous book, *Notes of an Alchemist*, when I said:

> The wind has stolen my coat away,
> my thoughts are becoming animals.
> In this suddenly absurd landscape I find myself
> laughing, laughing.

An alienated creature does not laugh, but a midnight optimist, even a fugitive, might; nor does a complete melancholic say, "the earth pleases me." This, too, is part of the record.

LOREN EISELEY

THE INNOCENT ASSASSINS

THE GREEN LION

There is a green lion in the bush at the end of the path.
If I do not look at him directly I can see the blink
                                        of a green eyelid,
                                    I can see
the muzzle, the ears, the face in the foliage,
                              green when the wind blows.
He blinks, or perhaps a leaf blinks for him.
                        I know I am nearsighted, see
such forms everywhere.
                  I have traveled, known animals, they have
filled my life for sixty years.   I am a throwback.
People write about the stone age, its magic, its meaning
                              or non-meaning,
                          endlessly arguing.
This morning, early, I saw the green lion and I knew the secret.
                              Listen, this is man's gift,
                          the symbol before writing.
You live all your life in snowstorms and brief tundra summers,
                                          live
with mammoth, reindeer, musk-ox, and the after-image stays
                        that is the most of man, that is the secret.
Somewhere behind your eyelids are established the snow paths
                        the moving game herds
                        the shaggy bison.
                        You old, you the artist, see,
                        see, even if half blind,
                        the looming mammoth.
The beasts flow on the eyelid as on a cave wall, the paint splotches
                                          take form.
                    The magic is in the after-image,
                              no more,
the rest is extraneous.
                  I am old now, but I see with the hunters.

This is the secret:
There is a green lion in a green bush at the end of the path.
If I do not look at him, he blinks.
True it may be a leaf, but I see him, that is the secret.
After sixty summers one sees life
mostly behind one's eyelids, the forms in the mind
peep out readily
as a green lion from a bush.   I look again.
He is truly there.   I saw him.   I saw him blink.
The green lion.

WHY DID THEY GO?

Why did they go, why did they go away—
plesiosaurs, fish-reptiles, pterodactyls of the air,
triceratops beneath an armored shield and frills of thorn,
tyrannosaurs with little withered hands, but jaws more huge
than anything that stalks the modern world—
why did they go?
     Were they
        in the egg vulnerable?
But then there trotted after, through green glades,
       horses the size of collies,
       gracefully stepping cats
with teeth like knives. They roared, they roared,
          and then they struck,
   finding the jugular like adept assassins,
   searching through aeons till they came upon, in turn,
   camels, musk-oxen, antelope, and deer,
also the throats of bison heavy-maned with giant horns.
Mammoth, mastodon, beyond the knives of even such as these,
      they also ebbed away as the ice ebbed,
as the first wolves grew scarcer, and as man, naked, shook
his first flint-headed spear that had at last outsprung
the giant cats. Why did they go, through eras, centuries, the strong,
          the strongest?
No one knows.
     Now man is master here with leaping death,
grenades, flame-throwers, the power of solar-flares,
        the force to hurl
missiles against the moon. Now man is master here, a dinosaur,
    Gorgon, perhaps, incarnate once again.
Note the shrunk arms, bipedal gait, contrived
bulldozer jaws, but delicately manipulating still
        with small dry hands
his final test-tube death.

There they all lie, pteranodon,
the deadly cats, dire wolves, cave lions, giant bears,
caught in the strata not to be returned.
Man deadly, deadlier, magical of brain, is he
truly other?
His seeming kind, the scaled ones of another age,
roved the wide seas,
basked in the sun, stalked, grew
invincible, while tiny mammals watched
behind fern fronds so long an age passed as though it held
a wizardry that kept all shapes inviolate.

Why did the lizards go? Why did the cats who carried
Florentine daggers in their delicate mouths
see fit to slip away? Why did the swift wild horses,
giant condors, go,
the finest of their kind?
Why did they leave the Gila monster, mountain rattler,
hooded cobra,
safe, still, within the night?
Man had not come with that all-sinister devouring brain.

Why did they go? Because
time and the world love change. No answer really, but I stare
and ask
what clock ticks in the heart. We, too, have come
most recently from caverns in the rocks. Our flesh is linked
to these
great bones that we recover. Have a care,
even in the symbol-shifting brain we may be
unable to escape prophetic things. We may
be wandering our own way on the roads of night, hearing the howl,
the guttural laugh of that which will replace us.

Soft-stepping cats, even the great wolves from the endless snow—
I will come and lie beside you comfortably.

[18]

It is the way
        written in rocks,
                the way
of that mysterious nature I have ever followed.
Only the cause escapes me. I am restless,
comprehend quiet, am prepared to sleep
as few men are, given the time when plants from the wild fields
shower their seed and carefree rabbits hop
upon Fifth Avenue, when all of us are gone, not I alone.
        Why do we go? The rocks give back
strange answers, if at all. Brother pteranodon,
I would have liked your wings;
        your lifted head, proud sabertooth, to snarl;
        mammoth, to trudge the world.
I am not sure I love
       the cruelties found in our blood
         from some lost evil tree in our beginnings.
May the powers forgive and seal us deep
           when we lie down.
May harmless dormice creep and red leaves fall
      over the prisons where we wreaked our will,
Dachau, Auschwitz, those places everywhere.
If I knew how to pray I would pray long for this.

PIONEER 10

It is the scorched shoulder blade of a hare
                                    or a beaver;
the cracks made by the fire are like palm prints
                                    over the surface of the bone
pointing the way to tomorrow's hunting
                                    and that charred cluster of lines
marks a rockfall up country and a herd of caribou,
things to be seen on the morrow
                                    inscribed here through fire.

This cosmos of a little band of hunting Indians
                                    has meaning.

Every rock, every stream, every animal
                    is accounted for
                    and the deep underlying
                    rhythm of things
can inscribe the message of the forest
          on the cracked bone of a hare.
It is true that instructions for getting one's food,
                    for hunting,
might seem the sole issue here and the shaman's reading
                              extrapolated
becomes mathematics and systems analysis
                    in the modern state.

But no, I think not and I envy the dark-faced man by the fire.
His magic is not small, he is reading
something permanently bound into his universe
that he can decipher,
          a code that can be read by the informed seer,
a voice from the universe reassuring for man,
                    hungry, enfeebled,
                         but knowing
there is a message to be read and one can find it
                    any time in the fire.
          The world is held together
          and man has his place:
that is the message; the food comes after and is acceptable.

Passing beyond the asteroids toward Saturn,
watched by radio telescope and directed
                    by the great computers,
          doomed to leave the solar system
          and wander the far void of the galaxy,
our latest space probe whispers its messages
                    among the stars.
A great triumph of the intellect, surely, but the whispers

are only of our own devising.   They are lost
                              in infinitude and vanish
leaving us no equivalent of what the shaman
                    quietly accepts by the fire,
aiding himself, perhaps, in understanding
                    by a small song and the tapping
                              of a skin drum.
He knows about the daily renewing of a pact with man;
                    we hear nothing
                              but the echoes from a deserted universe.

Quite frankly, I do not know how to judge this matter,
camped here in the spruce forest, but I believe I envy him,
                    the dark-faced old shaman
                    summoning Mistapeo, his inner one,
                              with a little offering of tobacco leaves.

THE LEAF PILE

In the yard the autumn leaves are slowly
               losing the color of the golden season.
They lie in little piles
        and the sunlight
           the last before winter
touches them and the resinous brown pine needles
                distilling
the illusive half-hidden
           apple smell of autumn.
Scholars say that the archencephalon,
       the old limbic brain,
       the nose-brain of our reptile past,
hides in the depths of the skull vault
      and that sometimes
        touched or injured
it senses odors
      from the night world of ten million centuries.
I think it is so now.
        In the leaf pile I have seen secretly thrust forth
        an indescribable grey muzzle.
        I shall not investigate;
        it is my own.
Smelling autumn I have resurrected
      what has slept a long time.
Be quiet now—
     let him hide in the sunlight and the leaves.
     He breathes and snuffles;
     he has been a long time in the black dark,
       scaled, snouted,
         incalculably ugly.
Let him breathe
     autumn;
       he is part of myself.

Through him has come
the sense of all these leaves;
he has rooted his way up
through dynasties of neocortex.
Let him breathe.
Let him savor the earth;
let him nuzzle the leaves.

DESPERATE I WALKED

In the November light on the drab thoroughfare it passed me,
silvering the grey day with its tiny shimmering perfection,
a small planet,
                life seed, thistledown,
journeying the wrong way toward the city's heart.
It was all alone on a slight wind, had come
many miles perhaps,
                and it brought memories
to me who could bear none.
                I took it gently from the air, walking
                onward for blocks, seeking
a place where it could bed for the winter and be given
                a chance to grow.
                I had a home once where such things
happened by nature without human intervention.
        Here I walked by car lots, highways,
I walked by pruned hedges, by formal gardens.
I knew if I dropped the seed its life would perish
either at once or be quickly weeded
                from all the delicate, suburban gardens.

I tramped so long a fear took me;
                my hand was cramped from carrying the seed,
where could I put it?
        I was like the last knowing man
carrying the last vital thing,
        the last feral seed nursed in his hand,
the last wild chance in the universe.
        Desperate I walked,
        a mad anxiety heightening my pulse.
In the curve of an old wall where the leaves
                were obviously never gathered

I buried it
hoping for resurrection.
The snows will come and the rains, but what have we done,
how have we come to this:
that someone, even I, must think, and not nature,
thoughts for the winter sleep of the last thistledown?

THE DOUBLE

I had a dream, a dream I had, between midnight and morning,
                                                    bearded, grey,
crouched in a horse barn, hidden in straw, hearing the stamp
of animals, myself one, holed up, concealed, the gun
always concealed, not on me, no, not that, rather the way it was
once in the harvest fields, and on long freights where men
hid them in gondolas among the coal, to be recovered
                                        at division stops;
in other words, dreamed the conclusive ending to my youthful years:
the brutal, battered face, relentless, wild, the fugitive
grown old, nothing left now but a fierce cunning, and illiterate hate.

How did I dream this dream, awake in straw, the barn,
the very texture of its weathered wood so real
I ran my hands over my grizzled jaws and brow? Then I, the animal,
knew two lives at once, looked on and measured them
with cool deliberation, no horror, no revulsion
there in my sleep, no pity either, knew myself far back,
capable of either, no matter really, sighed in my sleep
most heavily, felt in flashes hatred, but not of me, that caricature,
                                                    felt hate
on a grand scale for law that hunted me, outside and in.
I ran one knuckle-broken hand over my bearded face and woke up
                                                    clean
in the calm bed within a scholar's house, held up these hands
transformed, shorn of black violence. Oh, I had a dream,
                                        lived with myself
in the cold morning before light, as alternate, the end come back
full circle, touched my sleeping wife, lay in the dark
hay barn, or study, held both, for a slipping instant, equally real.

All this in age, felt no regret, having lived two lives
                                        before the daylight came.

Time yields us this, the brain, too.   Crouched in straw
I heard a mockingbird, felt dawn approach.   I, hunted, knew
this one last bond between us, bird song, rose and stole away.
Leaving my alternate in the book-lined den I took the road
                          into my final and most desperate day.

THE BOUNDARY KEEPERS

They have lived for a thousand years with the spirits of corn
and rain,
the people of Acoma,
they have outlasted the hunters
as they shall outlast
these United States of America because they know
proportion, limits, dignity.
Sand paintings instruct them,
rattlesnakes in season.
Mesas and sand demand boundaries, we
are the newcomers, impatient ones, the hasty aggressors.
The Indians
withdraw from us into the secrecy of themselves.
Long ago
I have walked through their lands, slept like a barbarian

in the cold desert night.   Acoma the sky city
                                    did not receive me
nor the rain spirits.   Down below in a drift of potsherds
                                    old father rattlesnake
                                            advised me.
I think he has an affinity for my kind, a certain tolerance,
knowing our sting is mortal and apt to be used
            but even to him we lack forbearance
                having no deathly whisper to say beware, beware where
                                                you tread.
                                There is a boundary, a boundary
between us.   This is the secret, I think, of the world,
                            the unseen necessary balance.
We have broken it.   We do not hear *nulla pambu*, the good cobra,
                                we do not hear
the boundary keepers, the krait or the sidewinder.
Instead we travel like tumbleweed in the Texas northers.
                        Somewhere on Mars, perhaps, or Jupiter—
oh yes, I allow for our talents—
pure silence will declare the boundary to those who come there.
Old father rattlesnake, older than the rain, advised me,
                        in a drift of ancient pottery
making a dry sound augmenting the silence.

I respect his boundary.

All I could get from disputation would be a few feet
                        of very dark soil.
I would rather hear the first philosopher of limits
                    sing his small song in the dust.

THE FISH AT PAUPAK

It was a long shore filled with sunlight and I, on the boat dock,
was bored because I knew man was the master here,
                              no doubt of it.
Far down the valley the impounded waters
                              paid a ransom of power,
                    in great turbines lighting
the cities of the plain. The tawdry village of dockland
sold lures, flies, fishing gear to vacationing hundreds
            yet I knew there were arrowheads
                    on the lake bottom.
A thousand years ago a trail had passed
                              through the forest
and the soft-stepping moccasined war parties
                    had slunk like the cougar
                    alone through the night.
All then was still some other force than man,
                    some other hand,
nature, the dark power in the lake bottom, storms high
                              in the watershed,
                    directed events here,
                    drowned men in the portages
            or scalped them in bloody forays.
There were events here, this is difficult, but I say
                    not turbines,
            violence in old ways but not
            trollers in motorboats,
            not the taste of
                reeking oil.
        My friend, the fisher, had left me
sunning on the boat dock, I, confident because the unexpected
never happens, bored because of the turbines
in a lake magnified for the sole pleasure of water skiers.
I was alone, that was what made it happen.

It was only a fish leaping upward in a high silent arc
                on a shore momentarily deserted.
I was faced the right way, I saw him, saw him
                in the fished-out water,
the great gar with the cold luminous eye fading, fading
                back into silence and mystery
                while the current ran between us
to the brain's mid-center, leaving
                residues of winter leaves
                fallen tree trunks
                the old eye waiting
                at the bottom well,
                                not trapped, not ever,
                                but fading in the under water
                                fading
                                outwaiting
                                even the water turbines
                                keeping the lightning's stroke
                                                in reserve.
When my friend returned with his rod, I merely said
                "I saw a fish." I did not, in terror, say
                                "the supreme fish."
Maybe the Christians knew when they made his sign
                                in the catacombs,
the fish's mark for something ill understood
                                but waiting,
containing man as part of his element, not the reverse.
Understand, this is difficult, that old gar eye
is in us as in water and has yielded
                nothing that it cannot withdraw in season
                                from the cities
                                or the trollers.
We had an unspoken exchange and for just a moment
                the forest was restored as it will be.
I chipped there a small stone in the shape of a fish
                                and dropped it for him,

a little offering as one might
                        drop a stone in the well of night
                        and hear it echo
                                   forever falling
                            in the lost caverns of the mind.
I think there are times now
when he looks out from me
                            rising and falling away
cold-eyed and green,
                          remote as I saw him
in the green lake water,
                            not ever to be gaffed or hooked.

THE BEAVER POND

A beaver pond is so much like my mind
I look into its mirror and I glimpse
what lies up here behind my brows; I see
old sticks entangled that might be a thought
too stiff to move; the larval dragonfly,
stretching new wings into the glittering heat,
one hour ago was a masked deadly worm.
Within the shallows hover tiny fish,
minnows of thought, one might say, quick to go,
leaving the surface troubled, and dead leaves
fretted to merest skeletons like those
kept in late age someplace within the brain,
leached skeletons of girls, nameless, features etched away,
this one and that, the pain all sunk below,
not to be stirred, not ever to be stirred.
A beaver pond is silent, the leaves fall,
one leaf fell rather, without sound.   This way
the pond accumulates, seeds sometimes grow
but mostly things lie here that try to work
their slow way back to the unreasoning mud.
It is a place of age, this mind, this beaver pond.
Into it I can stare, while thoughts like blue
great devil's darning needles pass, but where
I need not know, girls' skeletons, lost leaves—
what can one make of an old beaver pond?
Nothing, exactly nothing but a presence.
So, too, with mind, and so with God in essence.

THE SUNFLOWER SONG

When the red cardinal comes to the window ledge, I feed him
sunflower seed that's brought from places that I know
and he will never see: waste fields far west,
                                    drear country that I own
nor can relinquish it—my brain, that is, my brain that holds
this lifetime setting in a city street.   The cardinal lifts his crest
                                    and recognizes
seed he's never seen upon a flower, knows too how to split them,
flies off, and presently, it being spring, his voice floats down,
                                    "cheer, cheer,"
                                    with many other
trills and soft whistles all intent on shepherding
some cardinal lady into this year's nest.   The sound
comes down to me.   I think upon these seeds now being spun
by some adroit bird magic into notes that move
more than a bird's heart.   Oh dear God, how far
the golden yellow of the sunflowers now, far off as youth, far off
by twice a thousand miles, and faces lost
deep in the sunflower thickets underneath the loam.
                                    This bird sings on
high in the apple tree, the notes
sprinkle the ground like petals, like all springs
that went awry a score of years ago and twist the heart
with sweet blind pain and unresolved regret.
                                    I tell myself
it is the seeds that sing, that, without seeds,
the cardinal could not sing, and seeds are brought
up from the leaf mould underneath the dark, formed, shaped
within a flower's heart, encased and strewn
for any bird, like those piano scrolls we pumped at in our youth,
                                    the music sounding
all through the house, so here the brisk red cardinal
sings a bright sunflower song dissolving

the sullen silence of this eastern spring. I think this bird a miracle
to so transform a seed, but then I think the flower
also a miracle and so work down to earth, the one composer
no one has ever seen but all have heard.
"Cheer," I say it on the page, "cheer, cheer," my fingers stiff.
I eat one of his sunflower seeds and try again.

WATCH THE UNEASY LANDLORDS

Habitat grassy plains; jackrabbit, able to run full-furred
directly after birth; present status numerous.
Oh no, not really, not ever as in my youth.
Trapped against fences now, beaten to death by clubs
at festive gatherings, picnics, larks of ranchers, businessmen,
by little children taught kind nature lore.
                Ah well,
this is the blind world swerving to its end, all balance gone,
deer starving in the trees, cougars in distant hills,
small puppies, bought for boys' vacations, left
by loving parents on New England's shores
at summer's end to starve or grow up wild.
                I hope they live to stalk us once again.
It would be just, most anything be just
        to man who speaks of vermin and destroys
        as never botfly nor bubonic plague.
Sometimes on winter nights before my window
I lift a hand against the draft and judge if anywhere
far off, far off in cold Sierras of my mind, in latitudes that lie
                    somewhere above
the circle of the pole, pack ice has swollen, bergs increased,
a wind grown colder, a blue shadow deepened.
The Fifth Ice would be a cleansing if it moved,
but will it move in time?   The night blows on my hand
            but will not tell
even the method by which the world was changed
and elephants in fur once walked, and shaggy beasts
outnumbered my own kind.   Reluctantly
I close the window, know that fuel grows scarce,
watch the uneasy landlords, know
that nature is deathly in return,
        but I

have the impatience of hot-blooded things, not hers,
                              not nature's
sleeping bear's paw, a white polar paw to thrust
forth from some ice pack if at last she must.

IN THE RED SUNSET ON ANOTHER HILL

Ours is a craft the ages follow and reject.
In the red sunset on another hill, I joined them long ago.
I saw them first in pictures in old books
among dried alligator skins, curled ammonites, parched cuttlefish,
or fossils much misunderstood.   They were
not charlatans, not scientists, alchemists of the heart perhaps.
They loved these things, they loved the queer
twist of a narwhal's tusk, stag beetles' horns,
a white owl from some tundra flown astray.
Trash, trash was what they gathered; wives despaired,
if they had wives, and flung it all away.

Their scrying crystals mouldered in locked chests;
they never read the times correctly there
and least of all their deaths; worm-eaten books
surrounded them, sharks' teeth and stuffed mermaids.
The cult is old
                    and new as yesterday.   I found,
once in a hidden place so lost I knew
that only Indians had sheltered there,
the teeth of oreodonts, a square iron nail
heaped in a little crevice covered by a stone,
                                    nearby
faint signs of an encampment, all were gone.
Only the shaman in the beaded skins,
only the seeker for the times beyond,
had gathered these and gone his way alone
into the falling night.   With puzzled hands
I, too, a youthful digger, felt of them,
and, touched by courtesies of an old trade,
went my own way and left them, though I knew
not in this century would that seer be back.

Since then I meet such men quite readily.
Some practice science, like me are not scientists,
wear a disguise best fitted for the times,
                        walk close, walk wary,
the peaked cap with the stars no longer suitable; we sit
before a microscope, or watch the Pleiades, but we
belong to an old craft, wizards who loved
the living world, loved mystery, kept talking birds
close to their shoulders, never solved a thing
but lived lives close to where solutions were
and did not want them,
                        preferred mystery.

I know my origins from that badland hoard
of hidden fossils, was taught by one who cast
runes by the burned bone of a hare, believed
prophetic dreams and held a proud, world-shaking name
in science, but knew voodoo drugs and spells.
Forever after I have wandered
                cities and seas,
                picked up coiled nautiloids
                                nameless,
and to me impulsive strangers have each given
bears' teeth
                carved masks
                        the floating heads
of things the roving Iroquois saw in the woods
two centuries back.   These things accumulate,
                a beaver's skull,
a mastodon's black tooth out of a glacial bog.
        Why must I hold such fetishes in trust
                        as though to be reclaimed?
Science has probed as far as it may get
                                into their ways.
Long, long ago, I realize it now, I joined another craft
        in the red sunset on a badland hill,

in the wild company of a man who sat
    down in the dust with savages and turtles.
                 I know
only the mystery of objects, save
what I can keep from being ground to dust.
       I cannot bring the beaver back alive.
       I cannot from a glacier-frozen tooth
       restore the mastodon.
Ravens may talk upon my shoulders all in vain
          and students hear not.
         I am bound to those
who, when the great herds ebbed away, in polychrome
    sketched on cave walls shapes never to be seen,
              half man, half beast.

Yes, I walk masked, would have strange things aligned
    in my own burial vault, but dare not say it.
Yes, I belong to that most ancient brotherhood
      not often named because we once were stoned
      or burned, or hanged, or now
      suffer the ostracism of the seeming learned.
We are not entirely welcome among men,
        see in the dark, wait for the ice. I think, far off,
        our arts may well be practiced once again.

I, MERLIN, SAY IT

Under the hill, the poet sang, under the barrow,
where crystals grow on the skulls of serving men,
the old king waits, his will implacable
fixed on some deed not done, some wizard's augury.
He does not sleep in our sense, does not live
in our sense either, waits, keeps waiting, fixed
upon some deed, some deed to be accomplished
but not done in our sense, our time's sense.
Under the hill in the rock-chambered tomb he sits
where armor creaks, swords flake, beards grow, he waits
under the hill, waiting the deed, waiting to rise,
under the hill.

Sometimes he dozes in the dripping dark
and centuries pass, sometimes the great
jewel on his sword hilt blinks red fire. He stares
and draws it closer, does not rise,
waits, waits with warrior's patience and a king's
judicious thought. Whatever it is he waits for
he will wait, his will determines that, his will that waits
under the hill for Armageddon, the last battle that
determines all. He will hear the swords ring,
he will hear the challenge flung, yes, start to rise.
This is illusion, lord, this is not wise.

Sleep with the red jewel on your lap, sire, doze.
The deed has passed, lord, sleep, the deed has passed
while the king slept and steel from the great sword
dissolved its own pure substance until now
only the red jewel in your hand remains.
Its fires are out, sire, time is done,
under the hill, my lord, under the hill.
Let your arms fall, lord, you have won.

Here kingdoms matter not, stalactites glaze
the eyes of dozing sentinels, while you
muse on the great jewel.   Surely you have seen
in its red depths that deeds good or ill
flow to one end, that time is done, my lord,
under the hill.

Relax the warrior's grasp that would break oak,
                                    relax
slowly and carefully through centuries if need be
the tension of the terrible will.
Let your hands fall, the jewel of time fall with them, rolling
deeds accomplished or potential, all as one,
under the hill, my lord, under the barrow.
Let time, the time we waited for, be done;
no brazen horns, no panoply is needed.
Your cause, their cause, is won.
I, Merlin, say it, under the barrow, lord.
Your iron crown is rusted; we are all equal here, we are all one.

SOMETHING BEYOND THE STARS

These are the letters of a golden alphabet
untraced, unreadable upon this shell
plucked from the surf that rolls forever on this coast,
                              the coast of Costabel.
Collectors seek them, they are growing scarce because
the golden hieroglyphs encircling,
line above line, the contours of the shell
all seem to speak what is unsaid, all seem to be
                              thoughts:
something that nature would not record by chance
under the kelp and tumult of the sea.

I found my first one tossed upon a wave
and took it for a message I might someday read.
I found my second groping in the starlight
by a dim pool as an enormous tide went down.
By then I knew no man could scan such characters
or read such script, although it well may be
that man himself has stolen from these shells
                    strange glyphs and pictographs that grace
old gateways, or funereal bronzes buried
in ancient lands beyond the farthest seas.

I have spent many years upon this task
for undeciphered in my desk there lie
shells in teakwood boxes brought
from many lands where tropic waters cast
such scrolls with similar messages ashore.
Strangely, I know the cone shells all are different.
Here is a shell with pictures like the ones that Japanese
sketch on rice paper, stylized mountains, little figures,
villages that still might lie
beyond some headland on a rocky coast.

Here is another alphabet whose characters
                    are written in Morse code or purple ink,
others in trapezoidal forms as if
in this strange genus, *Conus,* some of whom distill
                                a deadly poison,
nature's own hand had written
all figures and all forms that man might use
by stylus or by pen or delicate brush, or once have carved
on ivory in kingdoms lost
                    in far Cambodia an age ago.

Why is it so?   What preternatural hand has written
beneath the shrinking mantle of a creature
                    lost in the watery dark?
                    Who, who has sketched
the little village lost among the mountains?
                    I stand upon the shore, the golden shell
lies in my hands as if,
            save for the failure of the memory, I
could almost read, recite
            the inscription that has baffled me for years.
I am not
            unknowledgeable in these matters.
I know and I have seen
            how the mind fails us,
                    I have also seen
in institutes devoted to the brain
how lesions break transmission of known words
                    so that a man cannot name
a simple pencil, yet when the word is uttered,
                    he nods and knows,
but he is helpless, too.
            So here I puzzle on the golden alphabet
and know it can be read
                    though not by me,

no, not by me
                nor any man of this barbaric age
                        and yet I feel
this symmetry is not the play of chance;
something beyond the stars was writing here
a book that molecules have set in place.
                        Why should they not?
For even we
                bring out of darkness thoughts and rhythms
                that ring the mind with music;
                        even we
born of the starry midnight cannot say
what impulse drove the hand that sketched a mammoth
on a lost cave wall, or that carved a faun in Athens
where form was seen to be
                        before the substance was.
Beneath the golden shell with written characters
                admit that all is dark
                        but, in the mind as well,
is a great void from whence form emanates.
Admit that, too.
                This is the message on the golden shell.

THE BUILDERS

Against the red sky through a ruined tower I saw
Neanderthalers among beams, derricks, watched them
kindle fires on a new skyscraper.   On the open iron I watched
November cold gnaw at them, red flames in a red evening,
marking the way they crouched with arms outspread
before an oil-drum fire, those ancient brutal men
warmed by the burning of a mammoth bone.   I saw
one stoop as though he hurled a thigh bone in the fire
instead of wood.   Their clothes seemed ill-dressed skins.

They labored
stark on a building they would never enter or inhabit.
Perhaps, I thought, this is our mortal illness since the ice.
We build, we built the Ziggurat, had babble for our pains,
built pyramids beneath the whiplash for dead pharaohs,
built colosseums and then died, ourselves died,

on the blood-drenched sands.
We build crouched under heavy logs, rivets and chains.
Our shadow on the sky has never altered.   We must wear
bearskins and squat with hands held to the fire.
We build, we build, but are not habitants, we build
great structures, libraries for princes lost in thought,
but on the skyline hunching amidst steel beams
our outline is as old as the first ice.   We burn the ancient fires,
winds buffet us the same.

The buildings rise, they always rise, but we
are left somewhere beneath with calloused thumbs.
Why do we build?
I think myself that we are mated to the stone, that we were born
long, long ago from caverns, menhirs, cromlechs, dolmens.
The creature on the skyline stoops and drags another bone
into the fire.
This building is a momentary camping site for men;

they build but do not want it.   What they want
is mammoth fat, bearskins to huddle under,
red suns to mark time spent, weather endured.
When has man ever wanted or experienced more than this?
Buildings he does not own, but builds
fire for his hands, rough talk, rough laughter.
                                        So was built
the Parthenon.   It stands.   The people in the skins are gone
uncaring, practical, so here.

                        I see an old, old shape
bent to the fire while north winds blow, snow gathers,
                                        but the man
worships in his own way, could not build otherwise,
stirs fires, places a stone and goes his own path down
into the dark from which our kind emerged.
Rough elements created him and he creates out of the selfsame need.
Ask nothing more for there is nothing, no answer, none.
A stone-caressing animal paused here, in a lost century
                                by a little fire.
Say that I saw, and set a stone, one more Neanderthal,
                        in the vast dying of the evening sun.

FOR SALE TO THE RIGHT PARTY

Emerald green tree boa for sale to the right party,
                     no triflers please.
Daily News want ad amidst listings
for Weimaraners, Great Danes, terriers.
Emerald green, one of the most beautiful snakes in the world,
seen in its proper setting, flowing like green light
deep in the rain forest; even in this time when the whole earth is
                                           robbed
and hurried to collectors via air, hard to believe,
                   but someone had it.   I
looked out the window in drab snow, looked at the curtain rods,
saw it quite clear, twining among the curtains, even draped
across the lampshade, an old urge surging up from boyhood
for some world-shaking Worm, some dragon gained.
Studied my wife, too, secretly over the paper in my middle age,
the pros and cons, how much I could persuade.
Should be allowed, of course, the house, be free to climb,
                         insinuate itself
among the book shelves, could be encountered unexpected,
                     unprepared—
so it preferred—could also hang in coils, its head wrapped up,
                  most precious gem of all.   I stared
over the paper, speculative, but knew
it must be fed alive, sighed, grasped the problem,
went back to Weimaraner ads, sighed again, grew smaller,
became a ten-year-old, wife vanished, hunting
in a lost decade and another time.
              Two wading in a swamp, small boys alert
see everything that moves, caught the green reflection
                       along a scaled
                    old dragon's back,
a giant snapper's back, never such a turtle
have I seen since along a prairie slough.

They grow and grow,
get mossed and ancient lying in the mud, but now,
                    all over now
they're routed out, they don't achieve
such age, such armored growth, and reptiles grow with age;
                              just keep on growing.
This one must have slept
                    growing in mud and light and water
till the last men with ox teams had trudged by.
"Rolly," I screamed, "Rolly Rolvagsen, good god
get a tree branch, there's wire along the fence line,
he's asleep, he's tired, he's so big
                    he's not afraid of us,
let's take him home," a snapper, mind you, that
                              could take a toe right off,
we barefoot, but we did it, did it,
an engineering feat so desperate, I shudder now,
lashings of tail, slipping of naked feet within an inch of ruin.
Pole under him, wired down, the two of us to lift,
carried him miles to Rolly's house
                    and there he filled a tub.
                    Rolly's grandmother,
Norwegian, pale eyes ageless, used to all sea monsters,
incommunicable, just looking. We were told,
                    later we were told,
the great beast got away, accepted it like children
                              never doubting
the stories of adults, cried a little
for all the risk and effort wasted, went to play.
Wasted, one turtle wasted; for what I know not. Why did I organize
so vast a capture, undoubtedly destroy,
                    though I did not intend,
something the mud conceived, something the sun had wrought
                              where now
nothing at all exists, no dragons and no dreams. I know

[52]

I wanted him as though I were a river god.
                         Mine, mine
out of the uncreate old mud, a century nourished,
dead because parents could not waste the time
                         to put him back.
I looked. I know. Hadn't we labored with his weight on poles
through miles of dust?   Behind the newspaper
                    growing ever smaller
the old, wild urge returns: an emerald tree snake in
                              my middle age,
want that as well, no, not really, just for a day
the green coils flowing over the pictures, over the davenport,
                              then I
               would take him if I could, but cannot,
back to the filtered light, the stillness, the great vines
                              and let him
toil upward in green splendor till he vanished, became leaves.
Yes, Rolly Rolvagsen, I was wrong, you know.
Mud has its own ways, they are not our ways.

WOUNDED KNEE

In Memoriam, 1890

I think that blizzards are something real like men,
if men are dust and particles, and if they blow
like shadows between the centuries, so do these giant storms
that tread the prairies down

                                   assume personalities and go
and not be seen again

                      but, in the seasons of snow,
there are games too great for men ever to understand,
there are games too vast for men to ever play,

games of the wind, games of the avalanche, of falling stones
or mountains poised in thought,
                    or games of lightning leaping
from sky to crag, games of wild forests burning
with animals for flames, or sparks on quiet breezes
creating holocausts that sweep aside
only at cataracts.   I scarcely know
for what they marched or what they would consume
                              but here
high on this pass
                which has a wide road now
just forty years ago December played a different game,
                              a game of death
with two men in a drift-stalled car.
                        But was there cold?
                    Yes, there was cold that came
straight from Canadian prairies on a wind that howled
like running wolves, a wind that carried
the murderous sleet from buffalo pastures
                    where no life remains,
the wind that crossed the dead at Wounded Knee.
              I stand upon the pass remembering
              the frantic labor at the broken chains,
              the bleeding hands, one shovel, and no cars,
the wise ones all inside and we trapped there alone,
no cars, no cars.   We made it but just barely,
                          luck and youth
not to be trusted now.
                    The wind is cold
still in that pass,
            the wind is cold
            across the whole stretch of the northern plains.
Luck and youth,
            here in the high grey twilight I consider
what tiny particles are men intruding
sentience and will into the streaming curtain of the night.

[55]

Luck and youth,
                    I do not think that mountains
                                    blizzards
                                    prairies
have thoughts for these.
                        I do not think the snow upon this wind
knows anything but cold since Wounded Knee.
I stand in memory upon the pass and feel the cold
                    clutch at my shaking hands,
                    my face dissolving in
                            the snows of Wounded Knee.
I think that something follows those who come
            too close to where man has usurped
            the blizzard's and the closing rock's prerogative
                    to underscore extinction.
The march of glaciers may be a cleansing
                            but in man
genocide is a pettiness.
            We can attempt but never play with dignity
the great game of the elements.
            I am glad for this survival
                        giving myself
                        and my companion
                        forty years to contemplate
what is being prepared in the wild furnace of the mountain's heart.
                    The rock will close upon us
                        without compassion
                        without hatred
                        not having noticed
                                its creations,
being immersed forever
                    in games too great for man,
                    ice, blizzards, the burst throat
                    of Krakatoa or of Thera,
                    deaths but not pettiness,
                    because not human,

something beyond time
quieting us in season
like a falling bird.
God grant far off no memory of Mylai or Wounded Knee
or even *Homo sapiens* unless his name
troubles the night wind.
One can hear him now, his death songs
muffled in all the snows of all the winters
in the world.
Extinction is an art too great for man, he bungles it
by obscene malice.
Mass death should be left to mountains, left to glaciers.
It should be left to the sand that covers
the boasting of fratricidal kings,
it should be left to prairie grass,
it should be left to the sea that floats lost timber
but never returns the wave-tossed mariner.
Listen, I warned you, you can hear the rising voices
not of wind only, not of snow.
This is the unmistakable sound of men in their own blood
here in the snowy Christmas of this pass.

A SERPENT'S EYE

I crouched and drank at the green spring careless,
        careless there on the tawny grass,
for this was coyote country, not the city,
          and death can drowse at one's feet and refuse to pass,
disputatious death in the shape of a rattler coiled.
He never buzzed, though his sensing tongue had flickered.
As I drew back on my knees my hand was beside his head.
I was young and the water was good in that bitter silence,
      but there was disputing death in its leafy bed.
        I was caught with my wrist in his face,
        I was miles from nowhere,
        my pulse beat to no purpose,
        not any more, for I was distinctly dead.

Every sound in the grassland touched me, a lark that cried
             faraway in the blue,
the drone of a beetle's wing, the spring that bubbled,
         the grass unbending
          from my wet knees, I heard that, too.
The lark sang on in the meadow, minute by minute
                the desperate hour crept.
Still he did not warn, he watched me in cold silence
     while slowly my hand was withdrawn;
              it was almost as though he slept.
The reflex strike was poised as I drew away and rolled over,
        poised but controlled, the great coil had not leapt.

Slowly the mountains danced in the heat haze,
            slowly I knew that I
            might garner my age,
but only by mercy gained from the universe
and granted to me through the slit in a serpent's eye.

SUNSET AT LARAMIE

Somewhere beyond Laramie the winding freights
still howl their lonesome message to the dark,
the mountain men lie quiet, wolves are gone,
stars circle overhead, huge missiles lie
scattered in firing pens.   Computers watch
with radar eyes pinpointed latitudes.
Gigantic cupped ears listen everywhere—
a bear asleep beneath a winter drift,
his pulse is coded, too; night-flying geese
blip by upon horizon screens, slowly we draw a net
converging to ourselves.   How strange to hear
trains hoot in blizzards, cattle bawl in cars,
think of the Chisholm trail a century gone, and know
beyond the polar circle other ears now listen.
This daft and troubled century spies and spies,
counts bears' heartbeats, whales' frantic twists and turns.
The background noise of continents drifts in,
captured by satellites.   Still far up in the crags
sure-footed mountain sheep climb higher, lift horned heads,
see the night fall below them, hear the train, and stamp
as rams stamp, vaguely troubled, while the glow
on the last peak fades out.   Far off a coyote cries,
not in wild darkness, but a haunted night
filled with the turning of vast ears and eyes.

THE TIGER CHOOSES

While the oil drillers in their tent played deuces wild
there at a table by the Coleman lamp,
                                        a tiger softly padding
came to the door, stepped in and circling gently
the entire party in a stricken hush, chose one man at the door
and took him out, away, bones, flesh and all.

A tale from far Sumatra, but the man who told
swore by the living God, he, paralyzed,
had sat in that same tent; drank a stiff Bourbon, told
the tale again in the hot bar in which we sat,
called for another while I stirred my drink, and watched sweat form
in retrospect across his weathered face.
"They say out there," he said, sweeping a vague hand
                              across longitudes,
"a good man need not fear the tiger, only bad.   The tiger chooses,
takes its time, but chooses carefully upon dark nights.
                    I saw it go
around us all the way; I saw it choose as we sat huddled there.
It did not pull him from the doorway as it could have done.
                    It went the whole way round
                         deciding something, judging,
padding, breathing, almost asking
for a fresh riffled deck, new cards, but then it chose,
almost regretful, not angry in the least, but firm.
                    We found the bones next day.
He was a young man, too, not old like me who might have been
                              the choice.
I heard the tiger pass close at my frozen back.
          No next of kin to locate, fellow came
from nowhere, went to nowhere in a tiger's stomach.
What do you make of that?"
              "I think," I said and swirled my glass,
"just curious first, he went the whole way round and by the time
              he reached the door
the first man smelt of fear enough for tiger urges.
              He should have dived and run.
Why didn't he?"
          "Because he held us, that is why," the drinker said,
                    "don't ask me how.
We couldn't even scream.   His face came in the door
with that far-off, that yellow-eyed fixation beyond time.

[61]

Please, no offense.   You do not know the way things are out there."
                                    I sighed and said,
"No, that is true.   I wouldn't, but then do we not all
                    come nameless, headed for
an abstract tiger's stomach at some time soon or late?"
                    "No, no," the driller said, "you still don't understand.
He joined the game, I think, knew it, lifted stakes on us,
                    without the deck, that's why
he went the whole way round so leisurely, looking at hands.
                                    The one who died, we found
his cards spilled on the table there, he held the worst,
the poorest hand."

"This is a rumor from the East," I said,
"and since we do not know
either the man's life or how tigers judge or play
men's games, we'll never know what held you all so silent,
                                    a great judging or some wager
unspoken but agreed upon at midnight.   Should we say
                                    the tiger's wager?"
"Put it that way, if you like," my friend shrugged, calmer now,
                                    "I wish I had
not seen that little scrabble of chewed bones
there on the path at morning when we dared to look,
nor that low hand of cards tossed on the table planking.   Was it
a gamble or a judgment, maybe better
we do not know for sure."

THE POETS

The mockingbird in the bush cries caw and caw again,
hesitant, tentative in the evening light,
he sits up close quite unafraid as though to try
his effort on me, tries it again for size,
that old coarse word from the high air
trails off uncertainly—caw again—his voice box failing.
"Yes, I hear it," I reassure him in the bush.
"A trifle faint, but then
you're not so large, you haven't got the beak,
the body for that word, you're made to sing."
"Caw," he says timidly and cocks his head,
caw in the bush, caw from a small bird.
A faint defiance.   Then he flies away,
typical poet trying a new meter, trying all sound
he can't avoid, born to listen and repeat
harsh notes and beautiful, whatever the wind brings.
These birds are sound-devourers, for what purpose
no one knows, or if there is a purpose, but there he is collecting
old sheet music from the wind.
                    Perhaps he's kept
notes from some vanished species not his own—
how do I know?   His line is very old, a dim phylogeny
much linked with wind and sound.   "Come back," I whisper
                                        to the bush,
"I'll sing something for you, you can keep it,
something about girls and leaves, more beautiful than caw."
But "caw," he says, still trying from another bush.
It's in the wind now, harsh, repellent, he must speak
what's in the wind, from the wind only.
                    "Caw," he says,
won't listen, I'm a groundling, caw has his attention now.
It's from the wind, like crows.

A mockingbird will tell you only what's upon the wind.
Tonight it's crows, with poets it's tomorrow,
a dissonance no poet can encompass.   "Caw," we all say,

                                                            our throats grown hoarse.

THAT VAST THING SLEEPING

Fission-track dating of Bed I.   Significance of
the Gunflint microflora.   Carbon datings lost
because of variables within the fall
of cosmic radiation, paleomagnetism in
shards of ceramic vessels, thermoluminescence,
radioactive counters ticking while one makes ascent
through time on dissipating isotopes
caught in enrichment chambers.   Can you wring
meaning from this?   It tells the past
translated into years, index fossils, too—
we may be such in some far future year—
locked in old sea beds crustal forces lift
in buckled strata; ocean liners trapped
with portholes of round glass, staring like eyes,
lost then, our same eyes, eye sockets rather,
spilled in the hardening sands of tidal estuaries,
                                        lifted up
into the sun on rising mountain tops.

We will be raveled into amino-acid chains
recoverable from rocks, a few words etched on stone
pounded by breakers in oblivion.
No human voice will speak and no tapes run
croaking sad wistful songs like frogs in ferns.
Que sera will not be sung tonight,
                    whatever will be
has been.   The house mouse, now transformed,
plays on the grand piano into which he scampered
ten eras back.   Do not bridle, friend,
our genealogies would read the same:
tiny to large, then gone.   Six syllables that tell
time's stairway ends upon a rail-less balcony
for all of life.   Can it be you find in this,

[65]

meaning?   I will try.   Can it be that you
seek solace, are deceived, the life force in you
luring you on?
                        It may be.   Still, I try.
Why then?

                        Because I know all this and if I know,
something within the universe knows more.
I am a pale reflection of that mind,
shaped by its mere potential when it wallowed in
algae and ooze and was, no doubt of it,
the Gunflint flora that we study now.
Its serpentine projection into time
makes the world-circling dragon worm that we
are only portions of, frameworks up which to climb.
I begin to span these eras and to know
things hidden.   I grasp all that went before,
atmosphere changes, photosynthesis, Volvox to man.

Yes, I try to penetrate the future.   Only man
thinks of it, if he does, but so does also
that vast thing sleeping in the swamps of time.
I am his child, think that my thoughts must run
in similar directions; lately we have conceived
pity and hope.   Take this as a sign infused
into our yearning flesh by that old sleeper
deep in the Carboniferous, now awake and tired
of what he dreamed before.   We are his shape and non-shape.
He dreams in us and reaches; heavily we sigh.
If we must dream for him, mark that we should dream well.
                                        He is
so weary of those ancient swamps, he sees
the future clearer now, pity and love he sees
cloudily, in man obscured by misty violence still.
I try to see for him, my eye his eye
fixed farther and beyond the utmost hill.

SUSU, THE DOLPHIN

True river dolphin, Susu the blind one, searcher of mud
these many thousand years, you must have known
the fishers of Monhenjo-daro, coasted up and down
between the docks of cities buried now in ooze.
You did not see them, your eyes lost in silt
before they rose, deep in the muddy dark
                            where sonar soundings brought
beauty and food unknown to us.   How does one live
in the long storm where eyes go out like lamps,
one's very nerves unused, dim lenses failing, the pure ocean light
lost, lost, with the waves' dazzle. Susu, the blind one, having strayed
into this sifting twilight, has created
pleasure, delight, and comfort from raw mud,
old mud from which walled cities have been built
on shifting Indus channels, Ganges oxbows.
There while toiling kings laid towers, Babels
of a hundred tongues, you went on clicking, testing
mud, pure mud, and found in it sufficiency and life.
Susu, blind one, blind river dolphin from whom nature took
the sight of sun and sunset, replacing them with echoes in the dark,
I do not understand your world.   I do not know
what power does these things.   I comprehend
only that we are kin, that we endure.
Susu, my brother, blind one, I think we too are blind.

THE BIRDHOUSE

For M.C., 1840–1918

Grandfather Corey in his dying years
ruled a small room where braided sweet-corn hung
among the rafters, seed that he husbanded
and planted in the lot beside our house.
Old master carpenter, on his own at twelve,
was brimful with a Viking rage that fell
on all around him, hated children—
they tracked the garden, I was one of them—
hated the jerry-built poor housing that came in
during the First World War, loved only steel

in planes and drawshaves made to fabricate
ornate wall carvings that now came from factories
and had not known the touch and care of hands.
Hands, he had hands I have not seen again—
so gnarled with weather, splinters, two-by-fours.
They were men's hands from another century,
sailors', woodworkers' hands, concerned with knots,
ropes, logs that had to be dragged and shaped
by men and not machines.   He took snuff
from Copenhagen, sneezed into bandanna handkerchiefs,
ate cod bought dried in boxes from the East,
cursed if I stole his blackberries, cursed anyhow
at all his dying world, mustachioed, blue-eyed, as if helmed
with auroch horns upon a grounded ship.
I was so scared I tiptoed by his door; in rages he
smashed crockery, swept tables clean if food
displeased him, challenged, challenged with that cold
                              fighting stare
that embraced all the world, grandchild, his kin.
It was all one to him who had known open roads,
mining towns, paths that led on.   I hated him, he me,
save once, and that made up for all the rest.

Grandmother asked him if he would make a house,
a birdhouse for my birthday.   He rumbled like cyclone weather,
spent two days considering, went at last below
to his own bench, sawed, measured, planed and pounded
for two more days, came up with a Victorian home,
windows, porticoes and all.   Placed it in my hands gruffly,
turned away.   God help me, it is gone with all my childhood now.

I look at Burchfield paintings, stop my car
before old houses lost in mining towns.
I was too young to know his was the last
Victorian house, the last grandfather ever built,
the last time that the chest of tools was opened.

[69]

"Take it," he said, thus giving me his life
inarticulate, tangled with ropes and saws,
violence of carpentering and old saloons.
In hard times he had sold my mother's pictures there.
"Take it," he said, and turned away, creative fire
unquenchable, making me marvel, voiceless.
Today I turn old books, live in a century not my own,
try now to tell how Milo Corey lived and built,
what rage surged in him and what tenderness,
find it all useless, snap my pencils with
blunt hands arthritic, lift them in the night,
clasp them in pain as he did, have no way to give
in frustrate fury sunsets or houses to my kind.
Grandfather Corey, I am wordless, too.
I cannot make one birdhouse speak as you.

FIVE MEN FROM THE GREAT SCIENCES

Yesterday in a room, five men from the great sciences
agreed that reliance on nature was now irrelevant,
that the road into the future must be directed, organized;
we must be further evolved by the careful excisions, incisions
of ourselves, the needful ones.
They were caught inside, I thought,
                            in a perpetually narrowing corner,
                                when they were really looking
for something beyond human cognizance, instruments and guidance
to a place outside.

We have not found it in the laboratory;
we have not found it in a billion light years;
we have not found it in the cyclotrons;
we have not found it in the spectroscope;
we have not found it in radar sweeping the horizon;
we have not found it in the stars;
or in death,
or in the life about us;
                            yet I think
it exists and lies truly outside or beyond nature,
                                        conceived
in some intangible way by her.
It will never be found
                        save in single heads
and by them unrecognized.
                        Here in the fallen leaves
                        by the road to a friend's house
on a dark lowering autumn day,
I stumble aside down the path to an abandoned quarry
                        and find small garnets,
                        locked in impenetrable stone,

I find
something as unseen and precious
though finite
locked in my mind
but outside,
do you understand,
outside this inside of nature
we are forced to inhabit.   But the getting through
is individual.
Nothing lies outside of nature unless she herself
wills it, but she does.
Here on this whispering, leaf-buried road
built by dead men,
I feel the past slowly opening like a door to the future,
but my companion is far ahead
and does not hear.
He does not know I am outside
outside for just a moment,
beyond time,
beyond hearing,
beyond sight,
beyond thought,
but like the strange red garnets in the plain rock
I can only
gleam from this one place.
I cannot effect transport, make colonies, I cannot direct
the pathway of progress.
It is
not in the stars   the planets   nor the leaf-fall
but it is in them
and by them, and rarely, as now,
that the door is opened.
I have lain in the place outside.
I can never go back and no one will believe;
the men in the room will go on devising

the hopeless means to get there.
They will never find
the road to the abandoned rock quarry,
and if they should
they will never find
the outside.   They will pan garnets from the stream
disperse the leaves
straighten the path to get there,
and the door to the place outside will close
finally and forever.

AND AS FOR MAN

For W. H. Auden

In the railroad yards, leaving the city of darkness,
      leaving behind the platforms and the cries
      of baggagemen, freight handlers, redcaps,
I glance straight upward at a wall that holds
      the city back from the passage beneath the river.
      Huge power lines are guarded here; they feed
the locomotive's heart and the importunate voices that run
ahead of the speeding train with warnings of war and death,
            or even love, to any desperate one.
I catch, before we enter the tunnel, light on the grey wall
            none can climb.
Far up is a small ledge, sowed by the wind with ragweed—
      ragweed, beggar's-tick, foxtail,
      all that clings where man
      has his dominion and nothing,
      nothing is ever intended to grow,
      and supposedly nothing can.
Man would scythe them down if he could;
      man would poison them if he could reach so high,
but they live, incredibly they live, between the tunnel's darkness
          and the sky.
This is how I shall remember New York forever:
not by the towers touching the evening star,
not by the lights in windows, not by lonely and driven men
shall I recall that city, but by the weeds
      undaunted on sheer stone and waiting,
showering their seed and waiting,
      waiting for the last train to enter the tunnel,
          waiting
for the last voice to speak on the telephonic track.
They will start to climb then, they will have had enough of waiting,
      and as for man, he will not be coming back.

I HEARD IT BREATHING IN THE LIZARD DARK

I heard it breathing in the lizard dark, the thunder, *Mü,*
choked word for muteness, mythos, closed up, the secret
hidden in beasts' voices, tongueless men
questioned by Greeks.   In wild lands
I have heard sounds circle my tent at midnight
pacing, who knows what creature pacing,
or an owl's shriek and flight.   Fire, you will hit nothing.
Ask, you will receive gibberish or the noise of cataracts,
from *Mü,* mythos, mystery, voices in whirlwinds, deities
lowing in cattle voices.   We know, have known
                              for many centuries,
our language is not appropriate to gods, beast voices
retain the mystery, elder things hidden in rough coats.
At night when guards are gone, the museum dark and silent, I
slink for a moment from my shadow, watch
the moon on the most stupendous skulls, lost genes,
                              coiled chromosomes
ever created, the very form and stamp of thunder, dinosaurs.

Mythos, my God, what dreams could rouse these up,
call the dread forms of chaos back, set molecules devising
the voices of these beasts.   I try again with the old root of thunder
mü, mü, the beast in the ragged coat, but the huge bones
stay silent, giant jaws unworked, unmoved
by human words.   Try garbled mute sounds, try thunder, try
the crash of lightning high in the vault, or silence,
just plain silence.
            Once in the moonlight on the floor I thought they moved—
mythos perhaps,
            some thin and intertwisted wire
that links their forms to us.
                        Try again that long and low
rumble of beast sound, *mü, mü,* that hides
the frightful laughter of the gods contriving

on some wild heath horned heads that may replace us.
I hear them breathing in the lizard dark.   Try again, *mü,*
and break the secret open.   Scream like a panther, do not use
a human voice. You will get mythos, mystery, the secret will escape.
No human voice contains it, try again.
But be prepared for that long sigh that bubbles
up from eternity.   Answer in syllables it comprehends:
wolf howls perhaps, some beast that threads its way
                         through the eternal night alone.

HIS OWN TRUE SHADOW

Just fifty years ago we thought ourselves
still at the center of the galaxy.
We love the center, whether in God's eye,
whether, as once we thought, the universe,
whether as an all-rational mind destroyed
by Sigmund Freud or Darwin's tampering,
center we choose to be, but truly now we drift
a slow lost way upon a minor arm
of one faint nebulae while millions more
beyond the utmost void all shine and spin.
Still from black holes that suck creation in,
to antimatter that eludes our grasp,
hiding perhaps some mirror shape we fear,
still, still, from all of this who brings form in,
analyzes, discards it, age to age?
                        I am reminded
of how this passion haunts our primate kin.
Once in a zoo I saw a Cebus monkey take
a little handful of small sticks, arrange them
                        carefully
in a tight fistful, all within his power,
lend them brief symmetry, then bemused,
not knowing what to do, cast them away.
How like this are the mental sticks men gather,
insect taxonomies, travelings of light,
trajectories of rockets, pouring of our blood
down gulping cell walls feeding aching brains.
Our towers rise, our words pass through the dark,
                        but then
we cannot find the center, so contrive
to smash our little bundle of dry sticks.
Arrange them first and classify, of course.

Cebus did that, then flung the sticks away.
He lost his touch, could not construct a world
with sticks of any pattern, only gather and arrange.
We are his own true shadow, even we.

THE INNOCENT ASSASSINS

Once in the sun-fierce badlands of the west
in that strange country of volcanic ash and cones,
runneled by rains, cut into purgatorial shapes,
where nothing grows, no seeds spring, no beast moves,
we found a sabertooth, most ancient cat,
far down in all those cellars of dead time.
What was it made the mystery there? We dug
until the full length of the striking saber showed
beautiful as Toledo steel, the fine serrations still
present along the blade, a masterpiece of murderous art conceived
by those same forces that heaved mountains up
from the flat bottoms of Cretaceous seas.

Attentive in a little silent group we squatted there.
This was no ordinary death, though forty million years
lay between us and that most gaping snarl.
Deep-driven to the root a fractured scapula
hung on the mighty saber undetached; two beasts
had died in mortal combat, for the bone
had never been released; there was no chance
this cat had ever used its fangs again or eaten—
died there, in short, though others of its kind
grew larger, larger, suddenly were gone
while the great darkness went about its task,
mountains thrust up, mountains worn down,
till this lost battle was exposed to eyes
the stalking sabertooths had never seen.

Pure nature had devised such weapons, struck
deep in the night, endured immortally
death, ambush, terror, by these, her innocents
whose lives revolved on this, whose brains were formed
only to strike and strike, beget their kind, and go to strike again.

There were the great teeth snarling in the clay, the bony crests
that had once held the muscles for this deed,
                              perfect as yesterday.
I looked a little while, admiring how
          that marvelous weapon had been so designed
in unknown darkness, where the genes create
                              as if they planned it so.
                    I wondered why
such perfect fury had been swept away, while man,
          wide-roaming dark assassin of his kind,
          had sprung up in the wake
          of such perfected instruments as these.
They lived long eras out, while we
          in all this newborn world of our own violence show
uncertainties, and hopes unfostered when
the cat's sheer leap wrenched with his killing skill
          his very self from life.

On these lost hills that mark the rise of brain,
          I weep perversely for the beauty gone.
          I weep for man who knows this antique trade
                    but is not guiltless,
                    is not born with fangs,
                         has doubts,
          suppresses them as though he knew
nature had other thoughts, inchoate, dim,
but that the grandeur of great cats attracted him—
envy, perhaps, by a weak creature forced to borrow
tools from the earth, growing, in them, most cunning
                    upon an outworn path.

I see us still upon that hilltop, gathered like ancient men
     who, weaponless, detach
from an old weathered skull a blade whose form reshaped in flint
could lift death up from earth's inanimate core

and hurl it at the heart. Whatever else would bring
        cold scientists to murmur over what they saw?
        We are all atavists and yet sometimes we seem
wrapped in wild innocence like sabertooths, as if we still might seek
        a road unchosen yet, another dream.

MESSAGE FOR HARRY

Harry, poor Harry, lies across two chairs,
head in his mother's lap, at five it is
painful to hear poets read, better to sleep, to know
their words will pass like summer rain, the light
be darkened soon, and Harry put to bed.
                          His mother comes
up to the speaker's platform with a book and pleads,
"Write something here for Harry and please sign.   I want him to
                    remember you.   Please do."
                    So, dubiously, after looking in her eyes
I turn the book, try to remember how I was at five,
          flee from that image, try to think this boy
different from me, I clutch the pen and write,
"For Harry, please remember me," and sign.

Harry is borne away, head drooping, half across
his mother's shoulder.   "Harry, goodbye," I say, and wave
a timid hand, but Harry sees only blurs, disturbing lights,
                    not known to him.
          So came I, Harry, in my time.
So am I here tonight amidst lights, voices,
even my own, but wanting only what you want,
to be put down to rest, to turn my head away,
to have lights out and silence fall.   Dear Harry
whom I shall never see again, whose book is apt to be
long lost when you are twenty, know this thing:
we both will be remembered and forgot: this is the world.
Say that our lives have crossed, each of us yearning
for a quiet place.
                    I think, friend Harry, I will find it first,
                              but no one there
will turn the covers for me, put me down with sighs, or point
at a strange written hand, or I be told

this is my evening's gift at which to blink.   No, Harry, I will have
to go alone and find the place with eyes
sleep-ridden, all by myself turn out the light.
Goodbye and please remember, Harry, but you scarcely would,
nor would I either at the age of five.
Father and mother, Harry, hold to that and let
the lights grow dim, your head lie heavy
on this old book: remember only that your mother
got this my signature and somehow fixed
herself, her love, into one line for you.
                    This you should remember, Harry,
at twenty, forty.   She was gentle, kind.   I did not know her name.
I wrote my name to please her love for you.
                    This you should remember, and no more.
This is the night light lit for you by one most nameless,
                         watch for it,
far on the other shore.

IT IS THE RAIN THAT TELLS YOU

Strange, strange, how in the end it is the rain that tells you,
tells you the years are done, that there is nothing left but rain,
the girls all gone, the parking lot deserted, or, in the fields,
                        there still is only rain;
rain in the night, rain through the open window, rain in the eyes
                        till you can scarcely see,
rain from the wars, rain from the past that kills you.
It does not drip most gently through spring leaves.
Rain is the world's intent, it lashes every furrow,
stifles all cries of parting or farewell
beneath the sound of eavespouts and of gutters.
Now bolts split, windcocks spin, skies open;
this rain is driving toward the end of time.
No sudden hush, no light toward morning ever
will break this steady pouring.   I depart
just as I came, at midnight, with rain falling.
It is the rain that speaks last to the heart.

THE BOX TORTOISE

He was the last box turtle ever to crawl across the Pike and live.
I helped him do it, saw him start, knew well
that roaring speedway would kill anything, so sprinted,
scooped him up neatly and raced on while he
waved a vague foot in protest as we made the curb.
                What to do then?   Garden apartments are
notable in spring for chain saws, tree sprays, flower plots
                                              where ladies
dislike old reptile shapes that wander by, all loath to understand
that driveways were not built for their convenience.   Also he
might very well decide to go right back to that concrete
roadway he had been rescued from.   He was big and he imagined,
had been instructed by his genes, in fact, that he was quite
                impenetrable, his information being
some aeons out of date, a message sent, a tortoise message started,
before man ever was.

                        But here was I, man, if you will, one man
trying to gather up these living parts and keep them living,
snatched from thruways, coaxed from snuffling poison, hoarding,
                a miser really, a miser trying
to keep the last old boxed-in life and pass it on.
It might replace us, no, just hoping
somehow far off all would be well again, these roads be used
only by sunning reptiles, hopping toads, occasional deer.
                                      We are all
distorted now, askew in our directions, even man, poor man.
                              I took the tortoise
two blocks away to where an old stone wall enclosed
a last, unsold estate with leaf mould thick
                              and half-wild undergrowth,
ran burglar's risks, swung over, dropped him, where I hoped

he would be satisfied, not find a way
to circumvent the wall, just settle in, sink down in leaves
                                        to wait
an age or two. So there I left him, hoping he would discover
his own true sort, his decimated kind.

Ten, fifteen, maybe twenty years ago, that was. I pass the wall
quite frequently, wonder if he's still there,
          wonder if there were others, wonder how they fared,
so lost to sight now in this region. Often I wish
I had all senses, radar in my brain, heat-probing pits concealed
within a viper's wicked face. I wish
infrared sniperscopic eyes, owl wings of down. I wish
nose like a ferret, all so that I could
learn what survives on this last island, this deserted world.
Where did he go, or did he stay, or is his shell
there in the loam, a hollow of dead dark
like our lost skulls may leave? I think
box tortoises are armored to protect
something that was intended to go on, and I would help,
help man, too, whose thick-boned skull has treasured
dreams, so very long, and now is lonelier. Perhaps the hollow
dark that we both share, tortoise and man, is best for us,
                    but can it be
that dark is all we carry, all of us? Is this the only secret
                              underneath the leaves,
the secret I helped carry so far in a shell, and is it still
the selfsame secret that I carry now? How very strange
that we should be endowed to transport darkness
                    with a lifetime's care
to some unknown, inhuman destination, there to set
our chosen boxes down as if we all had carried and ignited
darkness for some end in which we play no part.
Sleep well, old tortoise; one dark's parting to another dark,
                              both lost.

TIMBERLINE

In the fell fields where elfin timber grows
above tree limits and the world is dwarfed,
where every thousand-year-old pine is crouched
behind huge boulders like a rifleman
hunched to the earth, where even leaves must hide
against the wind that screams on naked granite,
                                   this is where one comes
to be alone; not just alone, to feel
                    what life is like when one must cringe to live.
Here trees crawl forward on their knees, stretching cold roots
upward, drag leaves after them
              upon a stunted body, but this effort
is not to creep away, but gain a summit.

Insects shed wings
lest they blow backward;
the mountain weasels squirm
forward amidst rock falls.
Everything
forgets the downward path, gives all, warmth, comfort, growth.
Each would climb
void space if that were possible, or could be.   They will find a way.
Who asked them here?   No answer.
Who sounded no retreat
before this age-long battle had begun?
What diplomats cried peace, there in the lowlands?
Who assigned this mission
to rise and trouble the galaxial wheel?
No one will answer, no, not seed nor root.
On this tremendous height there is no answer
save the locked struggle.
I come as night's sworn agent, cynical.   I see that life cannot
speak to its purpose.   These crawling, knobby roots,
weasels, like inchworms,
enter the mind.
Where is it the wind howls?   Here.   Where is it life speaks?   Here.
This is the final fell field.   Who flinches here but crawls?
I, I, against the stars.

PRAIRIE SPRING

Killdeer screaming over the flowing acres
of bronze grass now the buffalo are gone
make a wide eery silence. In the midst of crying
April has come but meadow flowers alone
spring up to greet her. No more the hooves will thunder
of bison moving northward in the spring.
No more the violet by wet black muzzles
will be cropped under—a long silence follows
after the flashing and exultant wing.

IN THE FERN FOREST OF ALL TIME I LIVE

I am an atavistic reptile, I suppose,
choose my own garb, pteranodon's wide wings
of scaly wind-worn leather, or the armored shields and thorns
of ceratopsids, spike-thumbed iguanodons,
                                    or needle fangs
of giant extinct cobras, but whatever I am I will
last long, long-lived, sleeping in the sun
of lost millennia.   I will not be allowed
the dissolution of warm-blooded things, mammal or man,
intent on death in this year's leaf-fall, no, I still contain
a portion of lost lizard blood, I freeze
in any number of cold midnights, willingly bask
with numb sidewinders along roads at morning,
                                    feel slit-eyed and still
                                    before the deeds recounted
in morning newspapers, would prefer hot stones to rest upon,
but most of all to wait; how to describe this waiting
to the importunate mankind of this age, I do not grasp.

It takes old blackened scales no longer present,
        mouths that flare with threats unconsummated,
teeth that can wait centuries for one rending bite, it takes
patience no hot-blooded thing ever assimilates.
                        My kind were not
clever, they stared with yellow eyes whose pupils
were not alert to change and so they died, most of them died,
                                    but still
they had another gift, they dreamed long ages out
on mudflats, or in fern forests overshadowing
the life of mind; they lived the long slow aeons
                                beside which Rome,
the pyramids, are nothing, older than man, older

than all his fingered, reminiscent kind.   Tupaiids, lemuroids,
                              not any of them compare
with the old reptilian clocks locked up in coils.   I shift
my hands slightly upon this desk and stare unwinkingly
upon a moving dial, dials of the sort that men
live by.   I mean to sit here centuries yet, still not adult,
                              I mean to grow
larger, more formidable, more thickly scaled
before my end, I mean to last beyond
all cleverness, conceits of mind, I mean to quietly ingest
time of itself until I hear clocks tick to no emphasis,
watch their rusted springs break, see
their ugly pendulums, with no concern,
weave eras back and forth across my face,
itself illusion.   In the fern forest of all time I live,
care not for centuries; this desk may rot,
my hands will still be resting here, not hands
but dragon claws.   Look in my eyes, you will see time, but never
hours, eras, centuries, you will see
                              timelessness beyond man's power to be.

I place a delicate vestigial forelimb, scarcely used,
upon the table top, attest this signature, inscribe
the document.   No one waiting knows
this hand was present with the gorgosaurs; I smile the way
a cobra might.   An anacondine wrench of the genetic code
                              might well have left
all of mankind still buried in the coal; it would have been as well.
          I would prefer, like all my reptile kind, the still
space between clock ticks, sandbars in silent rivers;
man's first mistake was ever to see time pointed
somewhere beyond us.   Break the spell then,
                    stop the pendulum, sign
this document with a scaled hand and no
                              dateline.

THE HYENA

Habits of sextons, voice a chattering laugh, but credited
with calling men by name; food carrion, as equating with
primeval man.   What does one say of such
old crunchers of smashed bone, old voices of the wind?
Nothing perhaps but this: they have lived with us
five million years or more during which time we scarcely knew
more than to pick up stones, more than to think that something
could be done or chipped today but not tomorrow,
tomorrow being nowhere, not visualized, not held
in the small brain of proto-man when tools were fumbled
                              and words clumsily
could not be shaped against a year-long need.

So in the darkness, in the moon darkness of first men you laughed,
old beast of night time and neglected graves.   Why must you now
when all has changed, all altered, lions even
slinking in fear of man, why must you laugh as though
the giant herds still roamed, as though men crouched
deep in dark grottoes worshipping the bear?
I listen on the night, moon-ridden, waiting
the howling of my own name, think it not strange—
five million years against five thousand, no, I am aware
that you can call or name if need be; brush shelter, hut, or grotto
is no impediment.   I will listen, come if bidden.
One does not lose at once what is ingrained by eras; I can hear
my own name summoned, whether, as some divine, in wind,
or a voice laughing, calling down rocky defiles leading
to old, old skulls I once inhabited.   This veldt
has long been known to me, my name been called
by wind, by serpents, *Hyena crocuta*, by torrents, deserts—
call it what you will—my name,
my many-syllabled, made-over name been called
in all the graveyards of ten million years.   Old beast, old beast,

thank you for learning it, if this be true as naturalists
hint of your habits. I will be responsive in my turn, this is a deed
we have enacted, re-enacted since before
the blue ice wandered from the poles, before
man ever thought to live in caves.   I think
I will be listening for my name again, *crocuta,*
                when all the ice lies chill and blue
with perhaps just a final light still glowing
deep where lost London lies, or Paris, or New York.
This is your gift, *crocuta*; laugh twice where London sleeps,
laugh once for me, or call.   I shall be back when the lost waters pour
in streams down Cleopatra's needle, or from what steel juts up
of all the Empire State.   Your need is fixed to ours;
howl in the wind; I shall be there.   Call names,
if indeed you call them.   We shall be there.   We are
contemporaries on an endless road, *Hyena crocuta.*
Call in the desert, call us by the names
of cities in the dark, or let them fade
till we use stones.   Still we will be what we have been
                until your voice is hoarse
with all our names.   Call, we will answer still.   As you will call,
so will we answer.   Voice against voice, ever.
We are eternal agents, not to fall
against a howling on the edge of night.
We hear our names in the wind's voices, we
know that the wind repeats our names eternally.

OJOS MALOS

The little *ojos malos,* sore eyes, the red flower
born out of barrenness and bringing evil,
reputed, dangerously reputed ever to be
concerned with desert fringes, fringes of the mind, locked thorns,
cacti, sticktights, things that never let go,
blaze red, rather, blaze in our thought tight-hooked.
                                        By looking on I see
forms held immutable unless they dance
in desert heat, mirages, wavering phantasms
in poisonous water that tired travelers
seek in the canyon beds, littered with bones.

Arsenical springs, red flowers, prickly pear, dwarf owls—
why should the mind hold these in disproportion to
green trees where I was born, and silver water
that quenched my thirst in childhood? *Ojos malos,* sore eyes,
I have looked through them far back
into a place, a house untouchable, my father's place
beside the railroad in a swamp where red-winged blackbirds
cried between whistle blasts and swung on reeds,
then flew, and others came.   They say that *ojos malos,* desert flower,
makes only deserts, but I see so far
I see beyond arroyos, splintered bones,
to childhood, all illusion too, no doubt, but I
feel the spring tide among the swamp roots still, and how it gathered.
                                        I would have
things change.   Harsh, harsh, uncaring, let the deep
flow of the blood go on, that wild torrent
never troubled by peace.   *Ojos malos,* sore eyes of memory, record
no thorns have ever held me and no springs distill
sufficient poison to insure my sleep.

TAKE CARE OF THE KIT FOX

A shepherd in the Judean desert
                    flung a stone in a canyon crevice, hearing
something shatter
           in the cave beyond.
The Dead Sea scrolls
                  were broken from their clay receptacle
lifted up into the sun and read, the words of the Teacher:

"I that am molded of clay,
*   what am I?*
I that am kneaded with water
*   what is my worth?"*
Nothing in me has ever
                            been broken like this,
                                        dispelling
the soundless dark of ages
                            by the bitter sea,
                                        revealing
teacher and taught.
                    In the clay shards instructed
                    for two thousand years,
                    waiting in the black hole
                        for resurrection,
                            I,
                    with the same hungers,
                    with eagerness to inform myself,
but contained,
                    walking
                            amidst great trees
                    wandering
                            in the grottoes of canyons,
but
        "Thou has made a mere man to share knowledge
                    a thing pinched out of clay."
To share, to be companioned?
                    How shall I be companioned?
I shall walk more carefully by the river,
                    engage the light with my eyes,
record what I see that instructs me,
                    taking care
only to be meaningful across two further millennia
                    so that when the picks of the diggers
                    ring on my skull

the dust they raise will already be compounded
　　　　in words which set one man to coughing,
and another to thinking.
　　　　　　At least I will have broken the silence.
　　　　　　Like a clay pot I will depart shattered
　　　　　　in such a way as to make momentarily
　　　　　　a thin sound in deserts
which by then will have spread from Judaea
　　　　　　around the whole earth.
　　　　　　"None there be," says the voice from the jar,
　　　　　　"can rehearse the whole tale."
This was spoken across twenty centuries.　Pass it on,
　　　　the desert will hear you
　　　　　　　and send the kit fox
　　　to sniff at your footprints
　　　　　　plodding over
　　　　　　the last hill.
Time cannot be rewound, but you are companioned—
　　　take care to leave something small and furry
　　　　that he may rehearse
　　　　　　if not the whole tale
　　　　　　　then at least the last journey.
Take care of the kit fox,
　　　　　　he will be needed.
This I leave to set one man coughing
　　　　and another to eyeing the dust
　　　　　raised up from my skull.

THE CONDOR

The great bird moves its feathers on the air
like fingers playing on an instrument,
the instrument of wind; it climbs and scarcely moves
                    while steady thermals push
                    its giant wings still higher till it soars
beyond my sight completely, though it peers
            through strange red eyes
            upon my face below.
Its kind is dying from the earth; its wings
            create a foolish envy among men.
Its shadow knew the mammoth and he passed,
            floated above the sabertooth, now gone,
            saw the first spearmen on the bison's track,
            banked sharply, went its way alone.
Its eyes are larger than its searching brain;
            the creature sees like a satellite,
            but exists within
            an ice-age world now dead. This bird cannot
            understand rifles, multiply its eggs,
            one hidden on a cliff face all it has.
Its shadow is now passing from the earth
            just as the mammoth's shadow at high noon.
Something has gone with each of them, the sky
            is out of balance with the tipping poles.
            No huge, tusked beast is marching with the ice,
no aerial shadow tracks the passing years.
            Only below the haze grows deeper still,
            only the buildings edge up through the murk.
Planes fly, and sometimes crash, but no black wing will write
            the end of man, as man's end should be written
            by all the condor wings beneath high heaven.

I looked in the motel mirror and felt a rind on my face,
my own face a stranger, furtive, my eyes
blackened with fatigue from the pounding thruway,
sick lines in the forehead, cheekbones showing
like death.   I looked at the vile black coffee
steaming beside me at the counter, like a cup
set down by another driver, myself, ages ago before he dropped
a dime in the phone booth and listened to
               something in the cosmos that answered croaking
before it dropped the phone.
        You'll not make it, a voice estimated inside my head.
The speeds are eighty and the cops are faster.
            It's too long, I tell you,
              without sleep.   Whereupon
the fish spoke sideways from my mouth:
"We made it to here, we made it
crawling on fins that frayed out into feet,
               made it
      while cool wet scales
         turned black and shriveled
         in the desert air; this planet
is something you make or don't make.   Quit dropping
      dimes in the instrument,
        nothing you hear there, no address
        will be pleasant or give you
        the road ahead.   Keep going, you just
        might make it," the fish said.
        I flapped the ends of my fins and left
        a tip on the counter.
Ichthyostega, the old fish, has made it this far,
              maybe he even knows
              a way by the cops at the toll booth,

maybe he has a word
from the squawking phone.
Maybe he knows, but I don't.
I drive with fins on poisoned air through the night.
I drive with claws on the wheel I don't dare look at.
I drive hearing that voice in the engine, hearing
the background noise of the thruway
bucking the cosmos into shattered glass.
I drive with fins, but why, why?   I've forgotten.
We've made it this far
to the steaming coffee on the all-night counter.
Don't touch the phone again,
don't look in the mirror, no one will see
what glove is drawn over your wrists.
If the fish doesn't know
the cops for sure don't.
Drive till you feel
this mind, this engine
go out of control.
Whoever said it had any,
not in three hundred million years.
Drive with fins, claws, hands, anything,
but drive and don't listen to the phone or the sirens.
Pass the toll gate skidding
years from the dial.
Count one million,
count two million,
five.
Gulp your coffee, man, get going, get lost.
Drive.

THE WANDERING JEW

Lemurs with night eyes so we might have been,
or, with contingencies among the genes, we might have grown
one with the bark of trees, green leaves, been fruit, oh many things,
listened with sonic clicks, spread glider wings,
never been men at all.   I bow my head
over this book, this book, curse the dark day
I played with rattles in my cradle.   Now, after lifetimes spent
in laboratories, strata of old time, dismembered
bones from this place and that, asked why,
been viciously answered, why do you ask at all,
chance being chance, yourself chance, who's to care—
all being permitted, violence, cruelty, lust?
                              I answer
because I do care, because flying squirrels even
parachute down chimneys, I have seen them,
and in a little drawer within a kitchen table,
faucet dripping water, make a small home,
sleep daytimes, harm no living thing, look up
                              with innocent night-time eyes
unknowing what vile monster peers at them.
All such tonight, I who am savage, ask a blessing on,
I who have climbed through windrows of blown leaves,
through tempests, cyclones, storms at sea, bombardments
of open undefended towns.   I ask
the blessing of forgetfulness.   I would relapse into
small furry things with eyes like these except
I have come far in evil, strangely, just as far in good,
would touch the creatures all in innocence yet shake
with fury for my kind.   God help me then,
being not one nor other, being, in fact, that one
alone, alone in forests of the world who still would hear
church bells upon the dark, who sometimes think I am
that one to whom a living voice once called to tarry.

Have I not tarried since before man came?
My God, my God, have I not struck with teeth,
soared with the vulture, glided with small squirrels,
lived in a tree trunk many thousand years,
stalked with the tiger, run with wolf and deer,
            despised and loved my kind
and if I, Ahasuerus, was once merciless, I ask
                        for mercy now, I ask
not for myself, I ask for all who fly tonight, who hunt,
            because they cannot cease
from hunting.   I beseech
                an ending to this strife,
            this climb of aeons, war engendered
in a star's substance.   You who bore the cross
upon my doorstep and who laid
direct injunction on me, I have done even more, I have retraced
the climb before the deed enacted there in Jerusalem, still I tarry.
This is a heavy cross, lord, all these creatures.
They behave as I, lord, every one is mine,
not in your sense, perhaps, your making sense
                but I,
I am Ahasuerus.   I have lived long, I love and hate
in all these forms, almost I beg release.
No longer, lord.   I live and I endure in everything,
            not least in man.
Long, long ago I saw you on my doorstep, that one time
I heard your voice cry tarry.   I will wait on that
until the stars have shifted.   I endure.   I am that one,
Cartophilus, Ahasuerus, many-named, whose steps
have worn the ages out before you came, perhaps was you
in shifting guise, the mirror shape who traded crosses there
upon a doorstep in Jerusalem.   Forgive if blasphemy,
forget if true, lost is the way we came
                    upon the road to Calvary.
I do not think this heresy, my lord.
We are joint substance of a star, we walk

together an old road, I am confused, my name Ahasuerus,
                              yours more merciful.
We quarreled, say rather that our shadows quarreled, and pity,
also a shadow, was casualty thereby to both of us.
                       Still, I have learned.
My name is Ahasuerus, I am stubborn, lord.
I walk with all your beasts.   I live and I endure,
grow in compassion.   Some, some within the dark repeat my name.
Do you remember, lord, or was it yours or mine, the cross we traded
under the heavy lash?   My name is Ahasuerus, also Christ,
               road-wanderer, forever and forever we are one.

NEW MEN, NEW ARMOR

"Gawain, Gawain," cried the Green Knight, "are you sleeping?
                    The ravens fly to battle on the fell.
Is all the Table Round vanished with gates sprung,
                    is the castle
taken by dormice, spiders, ravens?   Can it be that no one
upheaves this shroud?   What is it you can tell?"

I heard the knocking in the seed, the answer
from the cocoon that thrusts Polyphemus forth—
the moth with glowing eyes upon its wing tips—
I heard them all respond in the fatal north
where ice sleeps on the fern leaf, snow embraces
leaf, flower, and bird beneath a winter spell.
Sleep, sleep, Gawain, there is nothing, nothing that you can tell.

Gawain would come again and Arthur, but the ravens
whirl like black leaves to battle on the fell
where swords on iron are riven and forever
men's visor slits are emptied of their eyes.
Gawain, Gawain lies sleeping.
No one can find a way to make him rise.
Only the Green Knight who is Lord of Spring
unfolds the moth, the bud within his keeping,
but the great board lies splintered in the castle, Merlin
with all his dreadful power cannot bring
Arthur awake or lift Excalibur,
the sword that never twice on helms would ring.

Arthur is down, his bones lie in the furze roots.
Never the same men fight.   The ages sing:
>   *Gawain, Gawain lies sleeping.   No, not Arthur*
>   *can crush the Green Knight who is Lord of Spring.*
He scatters flowers, he leads young men to battle.
This is no longer Merlin's world, nor Arthur's.
>   Wild ravens rise and circle on the fell.
>   New men, new armor crowd the centuries.
>   *Gawain, Gawain, there is nought else to tell.*

This is not Merlin's world, nor Arthur's.
Their doors are fast against the Green Knight's spell.
>   New men, new armor crowd the centuries.
>   The ravens swoop forever on the fell.

HENCE CHAOS IS YOUR NAME

Radial symmetry, I think they said in my old college textbooks.
A dried starfish with curled arm tips holds
there on the shelf my old diploma, tries
to prop it up, but both are sagging now, the nautilus
just to the left has his own structured plan,
     and, in the howler monkey and the beaver skull,
I see my own bilateral caricature. It would be nice to be a star,
         stretch out

in five or ten directions, slowly ooze along
in rings of water light, but who's to know
of all these dusty shapes here on the wall and growing dustier
what would have fitted best. Certainly I would have to go
back to unmitigated *Chaos chaos.* There is such a thing,
       an amoeboid giant rarely glimpsed
compared with plain amoeba. There you see me really,
      old chaos lurking, thrusting out
his cell wall where he pleases, dreaming things he plans to make
in ages far oncoming, but is now *Chaos chaos,* will not yield
his shapelessness for shape, freedom for form.
He rolls, he bunches, he encysts, engulfs, digests, spews out
just as he will, from any spot he chooses, hates all form,
      withdraws at its inception,
rolls like a wave, an avalanche. Who would want
in such a body to desire permanence, stiffen into bones or teeth?
Resist it, put it off an age or two. After all one is,
    in this old uncreate amorphous thing,
the universe itself in miniature, hence Chaos is your name,
my mind's name, too, in secret, Chaos still here, still lingering.
I see these things upon the shelf, ingest them in my brain
        but spew them out,
spew myself out also, being *Chaos chaos,* restless, grown tired
of playing *Homo sapiens,* though caught in a tight prison,
       difficult to break.

I'll break it, though, being chaos,
old chaos in the mind with words to play with, symbols.
I'll have myself outside this cage of bone, I'll be away.
                    Just now I did create
a circle of green water light before I start to move and waver
                                        toward the next
fantastic symmetry I choose to be.   My mind is chaos
out of which comes form.   In the beginning chaos was, then form.
I prefer darkness at the edge of light, green water rings expanding,
everything ordered but in shadow still, the spoken word potential
                    in a small tree shrew. Everything that lives
                    exists in chaos who can take it back.

I mean to take them back this very day.
                            Enough of men and dolphins.
I will take them back and wait as chaos ought to wait until
            the right thought strikes me, but that thought
I, being chaos piled on chaos, will not, I warn you, ever be the same.
Last night I had a dream about green parrots, cacomistles,
                                        manta rays.
I may see in them just what I saw before tree shrews were men.
But what was that? No answer, save that chaos will
go on existing, planning with no plan.
                    I know that perfect plans do not exist.

I, being chaos, water rings divert me. Make a creature then
all water rings, green light, and let him think
my thoughts as they are given while I hide beneath
the pilings of old docks.   I think that I will go
                    back to the half-liquid light
                    before the deep was split, before form was,
back, back beyond hot lava flows, bird cries, to utterly empty seas,
lurk there interminably, have peace, be empty of
all movement, all desire. Try that awhile, let mind
delete itself, rest, rest. So ordered, done.

DEEP IN THE GROTTO

I have borne much to reach this thing, myself.
I know what only man has known thus far,
that there existed time before we came, and men,
and that beyond these men, infinitely beyond, there creep
poor old amphibians from dubious swamps and fens,
eyes in green algae, peerers from the reeds,
and after them small reptiles destined to grow huge
on roads diverging as our tiny star
                              circled its own way round the galaxy.
                                             Who keeps

all of the record from the wheeling arms
of spiral nebulae? Not I—this sun I can encompass,
this day's light, I can say it was here, has gone.
Back there within the dark there was a fish,
a fish that breathed harsh air and climbed
against fish wisdom up the shore on fins,
contained within that fish again was I,
perished but arose in reptile, scales to fur,
in some moon darkness turned insectivore,
part of me split to enter the bat's world,
the other paused from idling on a branch
to venture one day on the waving grass,
picked up a stone and threw it, gibbered words,
strange magic that whirled things inside my head
till metal clashed, swords rang, shields broke
                              and I
was also there and could not help myself.

No other creature in the entire world
has knowledge of his shape before he was.
On the dissecting table I have seen men pluck
odd bones, vestigial organs from the dead,
revealing their past road, just as old flint may tell

what heavy brows bent over it, mine too, for I
came that path also, buried what I loved
deep in the grotto under mammoth bones
in the red ochre that might bring her back.
Was it for her I wandered the long road,
I wonder now, faced the great bear, the aurochs,
in myself saw beasts, got lore from them.
I was informed on desolate hilltops, starved
for visions, slashed my breast; I have been many things.
One thing I know: that the red ochre did not bring her back,
nor flint laid in the grave, nor tears of men.
I have long since forgotten where it is she lies.
I have been many things; mark this, the magic failed,
ochre is blood, it did not bring her back.
This one thing I remember and no more.

THE SNOWSTORM

"It is the first and last snows—especially the last—
that blind us most," Thoreau once said, and I wonder
what he possibly could have been thinking since snow
is always with us and keeps falling
                              in its proper season,
the generations accepting it without first or last
                              save perhaps this:
There is a single snow which a child
                    stores in his memory, the first
snow when he falls in a drift, the first
snow that reveals secrets
                    like the flake on his sleeve
          always to be remembered because it brought
knowledge of crystalline perfection, infinite diversity to be tested
               with his own salt tears,
                    the immeasurable prodigality
     of the universal worlds in which we are lost,
     the first and blinding snow of childhood.
                    Second,
the view from the farm window, the last,
               with the black guest
                         waiting at the door
               and outside
                         falling and falling
               across corn shocks
                    wheat stubble
                         plowland
the whiteness of the void.   Lucretius must so have seen his atoms,
                                   created
out of them a world. A wind whipped the flakes aside, perhaps,
               a snow flurry that conceived
                    a farmhouse kitchen
                    and a stove,

made fields,
made animals,
made men.
Look, can you say I am not composed of snowflakes?
My eyes are filled with them.
They are falling faster now.
Suppose I go
outside and join them.
Could you say that I
was ever here?
No, no. The first blindness is to see the ultimate minute perfection.
That is the illusion of the water drop.
The second is to believe
the black guest at the door.
My friend,
there is only the blindness of a million years of snowfall,
and you and I
wraiths, wraiths, discoursing as we fall.
Do not bother to throw up the window,
snow is already blowing
the room is disassembled,
our substance,
the room's substance,
is snowflakes;
we are falling apart now,
we have re-entered
the eternal storm.

THE MIST ON THE MOUNTAIN

Through the night mist on the mountain
I see far away a light in a farmhouse window on the plain,
the mist mellowing it until it glows yellow
                        as the kerosene lamps of my boyhood
by which I first studied, the lamp of home far away in the mist.
I travel down the rays like a homing insect
      beating the moth wings of thought until
I stand by a drab house at the edge of town

peering in, as through time, at a little window
at the oilcloth table,
at my mother, my father, at myself
a child of five, reading a primer,
mouthing the letters.
It snows, obscuring the lamp until, in a Great Plains blizzard,
I find myself in a self-constructed Eskimo igloo
waiting with the family lantern in the yard,
for father to come up the path from work,
lift me and take me inside the house
to the warm flickering wicks
before a harsh electric glare had replaced them.
I remember sitting in the snowhouse waiting.
Time, why did you run? Where is the polished brass lamp,
the oilcloth,
where is the warm stove with the isinglass windows
by which we dressed in the cold mornings,
where is the old frame bed in which I huddled
with warm bricks at my feet?
Where are even the words of that time, some lost,
no longer spoken by living men?
Father, mother, take me back even though life was harsh
in the small kitchen.
Who would have dreamed
the universe so large? Through the mist on the mountain
I descend, beating the moth wings of thought,
hovering before the window
watching an hour long vanished,
myself, who never grew up, but simply
disappeared with all those others.

Can there not be miniature time? Some place where one stays
forever at the kitchen table,
on the same page of one's book,
with one's parents looking on,

an old photograph perhaps,
but that would have faded.
We would not truly be there.
In the night mist on the mountain I put out my hands
but the light is gone, a fog is descending.
I do not recognize this alien grown-up body.
I will not recognize it ever.
I am there, there, in the yellow light in the kitchen,
reading on the stained oilcloth.
We are all there.   I did not grow up.
It is not I in the night mist on the mountain.
It is not I making these pained animal sounds,
wrinkling my forehead.
I have rushed like a moth through time
toward the light in the kitchen.
I am safe now.   I never grew up.
I am no longer lost in the mist on the mountain.

INDEX OF TITLES AND
FIRST LINES

INDEX OF TITLES AND FIRST LINES

ABOUT THE AUTHOR

Child of the marriage of a prairie artist and a one-time itinerant actor, Loren Eiseley, in spite of the handicaps of poverty, was early exposed to the magic of poetry through the beautiful trained voice of his father and through his mother to an intense appreciation for the beauties of the natural world. The vicissitudes of the great depression led him successively from aimless drifter, to fossil hunter, to sporadic college student, and finally to a career in science culminating in the holding of a distinguished chair in anthropology at the University of Pennsylvania. Loren Eiseley's prose, long noted for its poetic quality, has won him among other honors the distinction of being an elected member of the National Institute of Arts and Letters.